W9-AZV-187

WITHDRAWN

Rookie
Read-About®
American
Symbols

The Pledge of Allegiance

by Justine Fontes

Content Consultant

Nanci R. Vargus, Ed.D.
Professor Emeritus, University of Indianapolis

Reading Consultant

Jeanne Clidas, Ph.D.
Reading Specialist

Library of Congress Cataloging-in-Publication Data
Fontes, Justine.
The Pledge of Allegiance/by Justine Fontes.
    pages cm. — (Rookie read-about American symbols)
Includes bibliographical references and index.
ISBN 978-0-531-21570-8 (library binding: alk. paper) — ISBN 978-0-531-21843-3 (pbk.: alk. paper)
  1. Bellamy, Francis. Pledge of Allegiance to the Flag—Juvenile literature. 2. Flags—
United States—Juvenile literature. I. Title.

   JC346.F66 2014
   323.6'5—dc23   2014014957

Produced by Spooky Cheetah Press
Design by Keith Plechaty

Printed in China 62

SCHOLASTIC, CHILDREN'S PRESS, ROOKIE READ ABOUT®, and associated logos
are trademarks and/or registered trademarks of Scholastic Inc.

1 2 3 4 5 6 7 8 9 10 R 24 23 22 21 20 19 18 17 16 15

Photographs ©: Alamy Images: 28 right (Dennis MacDonald), 27 (H. Mark Weidman
Photography), 7 top (Nikreates), 7 bottom (Tim Gainey); AP Images/Paul Sakuma: 19, 31
center top; Corbis Images/Bettmann: 24, 29 top; Dreamstime/I. Pilon: 15; Getty Images: 20
(Linda Davidson/ The Washington Post), 12 (Spencer Platt); Library of Congress: 29 bottom;
Media Bakery: 3 top right, 4, 31 top (Comstock), 30 background (Keith Levit), cover (Thinkstock);
Newscom: 8 (Bellamy Family/Sacramento Bee), 3 bottom, 23, 31 bottom (Tetra Images);
The Granger Collection: 16; The Image Works/Newagen Archive: 11; Thinkstock/Mike Kiev: 31
center bottom; Wikimedia/Beinecke Library: 3 top left, 28 left.

Table of Contents

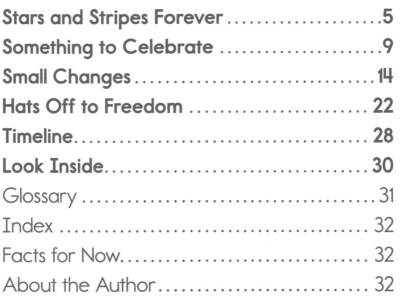

Stars and Stripes Forever

Millions of American students start their school day the same way—by saying the Pledge of Allegiance.

A pledge is a promise. Allegiance means loyalty. The Pledge of Allegiance is a promise to America and its flag.

Every part of the flag stands for something. The 13 stripes stand for the 13 colonies that later became the first 13 states. The stars represent the 50 states that make up the country today.

FUN FACT!

The first U.S. flag had only 13 stars because there were originally only 13 states in the country.

first flag

flag today

7

8

Something to Celebrate

The man who wrote the Pledge was a minister named Francis Bellamy. The owner of *The Youth's Companion* magazine belonged to Bellamy's church. He liked the minister's sermons. He hired Bellamy to write for his popular magazine.

Francis Bellamy poses with his grandson John.

October 12, 1892, was the 400th anniversary of Christopher Columbus's arrival in America. President Benjamin Harrison said everyone in the country should celebrate.

Columbus arrives in the New World.

11

These people are riding on a float in a Columbus Day parade.

Bellamy wrote a **patriotic** program for schools to use for the Columbus Day celebration. It was printed in *The Youth's Companion.* The program included a salute to the flag.

FUN FACT!

Francis Bellamy took two hours to write the original 22-word Pledge. He spent weeks thinking about it before he even started writing.

Small Changes

Events like the Revolutionary War and the Civil War inspired Bellamy to write:

*I pledge allegiance to my flag and the Republic for which it stands—one Nation **indivisible**—with liberty and justice for all.*

The Revolutionary War turned 13 English colonies into one free nation.

A Map
UNITED
AMER
with Par
ADJOINING
from the lates

After hearing the Pledge recited, Bellamy added a 23rd word, "And *to* the Republic for which it stands."

In 1898, New York became the first state to require students to recite the Pledge in school. Other states followed.

Students in a New York City school say the Pledge in 1892.

In 1923 and 1924, another change was made. People wanted to make sure the Pledge was about the American flag only. Instead of "my flag" the Pledge now says, "to the flag of the United States of America."

FUN FACT!

When **immigrants** become U.S. **citizens**, they recite the Pledge of Allegiance.

Fifty years after it was written, the Pledge was made part of the National Flag Code. The Flag Code describes the correct ways to display and handle the flag, like when to fly it and how to fold it.

By 1942, the Pledge had spread from schools to other public places.

U.S. senators recite the Pledge at the start of each workday.

Hats Off to Freedom

Military men and women salute the flag when they say the Pledge.

Other people face the flag with their right hand over their heart. If they are wearing a hat, they take it off when they say the Pledge.

These are the nine judges of the U.S. Supreme Court who decided that students do not have to say the Pledge.

In 1943, the U.S. Supreme Court decided that students did not have to say the Pledge of Allegiance in school if they did not want to. Many students choose to do so anyway.

In 1954, President Dwight D. Eisenhower added the words "under God" after "one nation."

FUN FACT!

Supreme Court judges decide the most important legal cases in the country.

The Pledge began as a salute for schoolchildren. Now many adults recite the Pledge, too.

Americans use the Pledge to remind them of their love for a great nation.

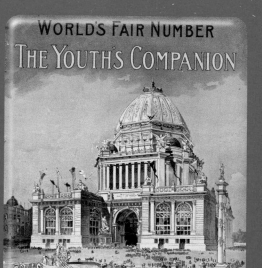

1892
The Pledge is published in *The Youth's Companion*.

1942
The Pledge becomes part of the National Flag Code.

1923
National Flag Conference makes the first text change.

1924
National Flag Conference makes the second text change.

1943

The Supreme Court rules that students are not required to say the Pledge.

1954

President Eisenhower adds "under God" to the Pledge.

29

The Pledge of Allegiance

I pledge allegiance

to the flag

of the United States of America

and to the Republic

for which it stands,

one nation

under God,

indivisible,

with liberty and justice

for all.

I promise to be true.

The United States is a republic. Its citizens vote for their leaders.

The belief that the United States can never be split apart.

Every citizen is free and will be treated fairly.

Glossary

citizens (SIT-i-zuhns): members of a certain country with rights, like the right to vote

immigrants (IM-uh-gruhnts): people who move from one country to become citizens of another

indivisible (in-duh-VIZ-uh-buhl): cannot be divided or broken into separate parts

patriotic (PAY-tree-aht-ic): showing a deep love of country

Index

Facts for Now

Visit this Scholastic Web site for more information on the Pledge of Allegiance:
www.factsfornow.scholastic.com
Enter the keywords **Pledge of Allegiance**

About the Author

Justine Fontes and her husband, Ron, hope to write 1,001 terrific tales. So far, they have penned over 700 children's books! They live in a quiet corner of Maine with three happy cats.